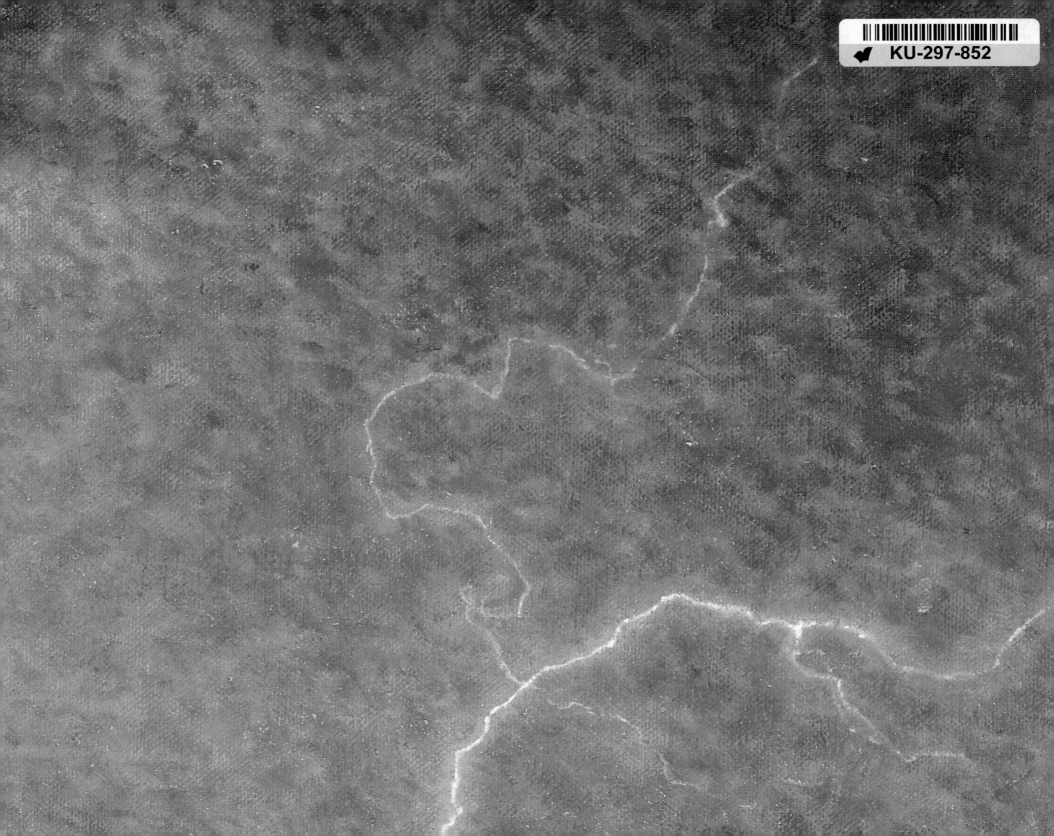

For T.W. D.S.
To Lin, with love G.B.

First published in 1993

1 3 5 7 9 10 8 6 4 2

Dyan Sheldon and Gary Blythe have asserted their rights under
the Copyright, Designs and Patents Act, 1988
to be identified as the author and illustrator of this work.

First published in the United Kingdom in 1993 by
Hutchinson Children's Books
Random House UK Limited
20 Vauxhall Bridge Road, London SW1V 2SA

Random House Australia (Pty) Limited
20 Alfred Street, Milsons Point, Sydney,
New South Wales 2061, Australia

Random House New Zealand Limited
18 Poland Road, Glenfield
Auckland 10, New Zealand

Random House South Africa (Pty) Limited
PO Box 337, Bergvlei 2012, South Africa

Random House UK Limited Reg. No. 954009

A CIP catalogue for this book
is available from the British Library
ISBN 0 09 176141 7

Printed in Singapore
by Tien Wah Press (Pte) Ltd

THE GARDEN

Story by Dyan Sheldon

Illustrations by Gary Blythe

HUTCHINSON

London Sydney Auckland Johannesburg

Jenny found a stone while she was digging in the garden. It was dark and rough and came to a point. She had never seen anything quite like it before.

'Look at this,' said Jenny. 'I think it must be a magic stone.'

Jenny's mother smiled. 'That's not a magic stone. It's a flint.' She touched it with her finger. 'It might even be an arrowhead. It could be hundreds of years old.'

Jenny looked around the garden. There were beds of flowers against the fence, and a fish pond in one corner. In the middle of the lawn there were a swing set and a barbecue. Beyond the garden there were houses and street lights and busy roads; and beyond them the stores of the town and the buildings of the city.

'What was it like here hundreds of years ago?' asked Jenny.

Her mother took the stone and turned it over in her hand.

'There were none of the things you see here now,' she said.

Jenny stared beyond the garden, but it was hard to imagine what it must have been like when there were forests instead of cities, and fields instead of towns.

But then, far in the distance, Jenny saw a man on horseback, looking as though he might ride into the clouds. She blinked and the man disappeared.

Jenny turned back to her mother. 'I thought I saw an Indian brave just then,' she told her. 'He was crossing the plains on his pony.'

Jenny's mother handed her the piece of flint and they talked of how the world had been when the land was large and as open as the sky, of hunting on the plains and in the mountains and forests, of singing, and telling stories in the firelight.

'There's little left of that way of life now,' her mother sighed.

'There's still my arrow-head,' said Jenny.

'Yes,' agreed her mother. 'There's still your arrowhead.'

Jenny stayed in the garden all afternoon. She tried to imagine people walking with their dogs and riding their horses across the faraway hills.

But all she saw were cars and trucks racing along the busy road.

She tried to picture young men hunting in the high grass of the plains, their movements slow and their weapons ready.

But all she saw was the cat stalking through the flowers and her mother's shrubs.

As dusk blurred the shapes in the garden, Jenny almost thought she heard women bent over their fires, their voices soft and laughing.

But it was only the radio in the house next door.

Jenny was still outside when the moon came up.

'Jenny!' called her mother from the house. 'Come on in, it's getting dark.'

But Jenny pretended not to hear. She wanted to stay where she was, watching in the garden.

Later, she asked if she could sleep in her tent, the way people used to.

Jenny's mother sighed. 'All right,' she said. 'But we must put your tent close to the house so I can keep an eye on you.'

Jenny lay awake for a long time that night. She listened for the howling of the wolves and gazed out at the stars. She stared at the sky so hard that she thought she saw a trail of clouds turn into buffalo and race across the moon. When finally she did fall asleep, the arrowhead was still fast in her hand.

J enny had a dream.
She dreamt that she woke
in the night.

From somewhere close by
came the murmur of low
voices. She cautiously
opened the flap of her tent.

The world outside had
changed.

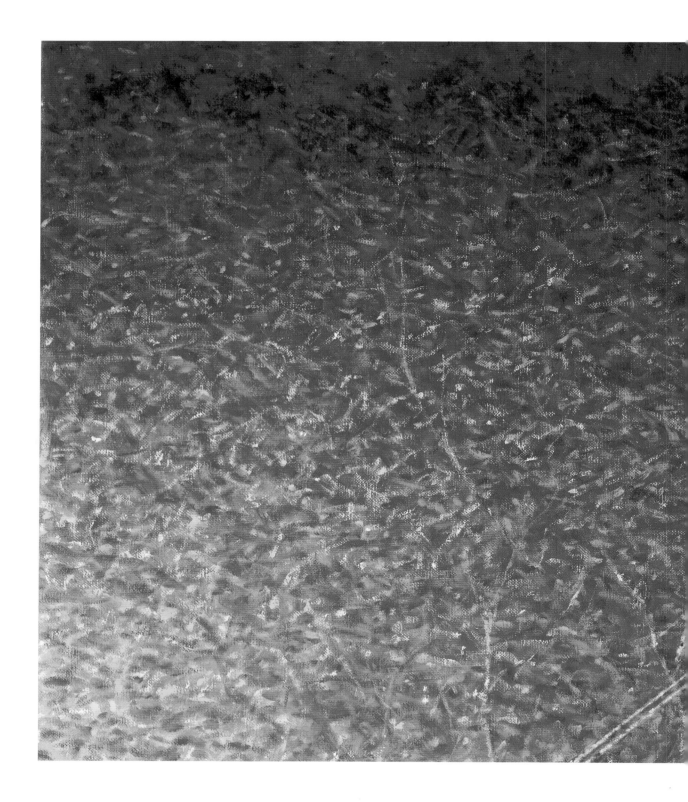

The moon was corn-yellow and the stars sat low in a blue-black sky.

There were no houses or lights, no roads and no cars. Where the city had been there were only hills. Where the town had stood were fields of grass. Night birds called and the trees rustled. Jenny's garden was gone.

She looked around in wonder. There were ponies where the vegetable patch should have been, and dogs dozing where the flowers had grown. In place of the fish pond was a whispering stream. Instead of the swing set, painted tipis stood in a clearing, smoke drifting past them like clouds. And there, where the barbecue had been, a circle of people sat round a fire, their voices soft.

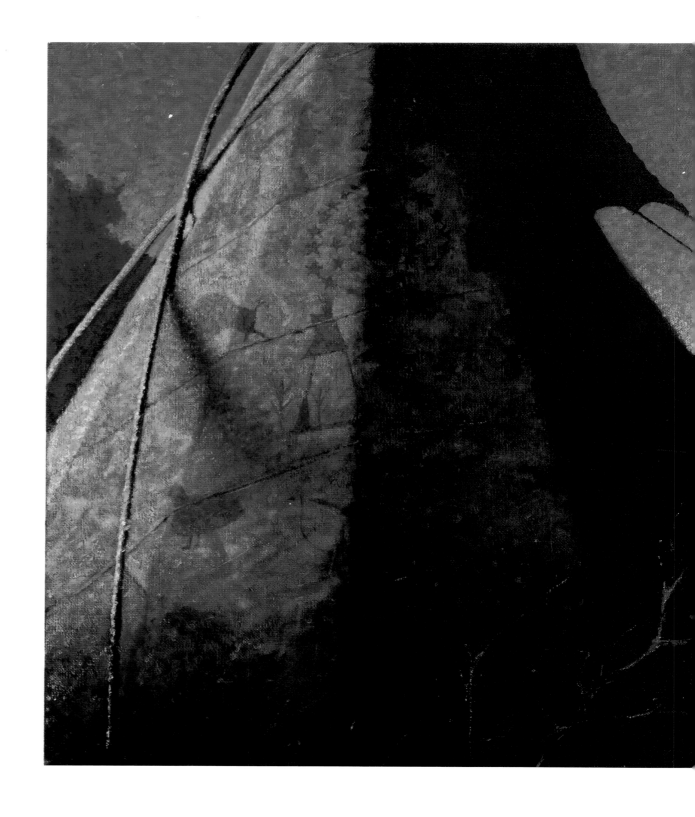

One of the men turned and looked towards Jenny. He beckoned her over.

Because it was a dream, Jenny knew what he wanted. He wanted her to return his stone.

The dogs began to bark as Jenny crawled from her tent, but because she was dreaming she wasn't afraid. She crossed to the fire.

The man moved over and Jenny sat down. She placed the arrowhead into his hand.

Jenny sat with the Indians all through the night, while the drum played, and the flute sounded, and they told her how the world had been, so long ago, when the land was large. When there were stories in the stars and songs in the sun. When every thing on earth had a voice and a heart, and time was measured by the changings of the moon.

In the morning, when Jenny really woke up, the world was as it always was again. The flowers were still growing along the fence. The cars were still speeding past on the busy road. The arrowhead was still in her hand.

Jenny stared beyond the yard. Clouds drifted past the sun like smoke. The beating of her heart recalled the drumming of her dream.

Without a sound, Jenny crept from her tent. At the edge of the garden she knelt in the grass, and buried the arrowhead back in the earth.

She looked up at the sky. And just for an instant, in the shimmering light, she saw the world as it once was, so long ago, when the land was large.